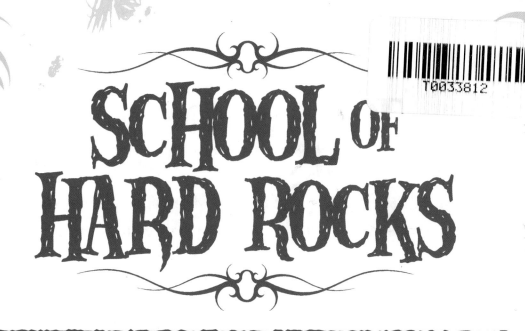

SCHOOL OF HARD ROCKS

A WORKING DRUMMER'S GUIDE TO REAL-WORLD DRUMMING

BY BART ROBLEY

ISBN 978-1-57424-238-6
SAN 683-8022

Book Design by Roy David Dains / London West Advertising
www.londonwestadvertising.com

Copyright © 2008 CENTERSTREAM Publishing, LLC
P.O. Box 17878 - Anaheim Hills, CA 92817

www.centerstream-usa.com

FOREWORD

Bart and I met in the spring of 1994 and the musical chemistry between us was obvious from the first day of jamming together. Realizing that we shared a common vision, we decided to join forces to form a Heavy Metal trio called War Crime. With the release of two Cds: War Crime "Live" and "No Escape", the band played the L.A. club scene extensively, winning over Metal fans one gig at a time. By 1998 the Metal scene had changed drastically and we decided to give the metal beast a break to pursue other projects.

I decided it was time to produce a solo CD titled "Dissolution" and Bart shifted gears to join Southern Rockers, The Sam Morrison Band. Well, as destiny would have it, their guitarist walked out half way through a show and that's when I got the call from Bart asking me to "sit in". I hesitantly accepted because I was unfamiliar with their repertoire and the songs in general. However, the remainder of the show went off unexpectedly well and the rest is history.

We continue to perform together today and I can honestly say that Bart Robley is one of the best drummers I have ever played with, hands down. His extensive knowledge and rhythmic insight is sure to inspire young upstarts and seasoned players alike.

There is much knowledge to be absorbed within these pages and well worth the study. Sacrifice and discipline is what it takes to rise above mediocrity. My best of luck to all fellow musicians who can express true emotion from the sound of their instrument. Only you have the ability to release the untapped symphony within your soul.

Never Say Die!

Steven Cenker

www.stevencenker.com

BART ROBLEY's

SCHOOL OF HARD ROCKS

I N T R O D U C T I O N

Playing drums has been the driving force in my life. I am fortunate to have found a way to make a living doing something I love. I consider myself a "blue collar drummer," because I dabble in a bit of everything. I play in bands, teach, do studio work, write for a drum magazine, and now authored this book.

When learning to play the drums or any musical instrument you have to be patient with yourself, take your time, and go step-by-step. I recommend finding a private instructor. A good instructor can help you understand and eliminate some of the guess work in reading music. They can also help you with your technique by pointing out what you might be doing wrong and get you on track. A good instructor can be very motivational and help you build good practice habits.

I've put this book together in such a fashion that each step will build on the next. When you get through the final section, your playing should come together into rhythms that can be useful in many playing situations.

Happy Drumming!

Bart Robley

MUSIC RISES FROM THE HUMAN HEART.
WHEN THE EMOTIONS ARE TOUCHED,
THEY ARE EXPRESSED IN SOUNDS,
AND WHEN THE SOUNDS TAKE ON FORMS,
WE HAVE MUSIC.
Chinese Classic

BART ROBLEY's
SCHOOL OF
HARD ROCKS

TABLE OF CONTENTS

Introduction   3

Key   6

Section 1   -   Introduction to Rhythm   7

Section 2   -   Eighth Note Triplets   14

Section 3   -   Rebound Strokes   21

Section 4   -   Rebound Sixteenth Notes   23

Section 5   -   Warm-Up Exercise   25

Section 6   -   Accented Sixteenth Notes   27

Section 7   -   Accented Sixteenth Notes with Bass Drum   31

Section 8   -   Accented Sixteenth Notes with Hi-Hat and Bass Drum   35

Section 9   -   Accented Eighth Note Triplets   39

Section 10   -   Accented Eighth Note Triplets with Bass Drum   42

Section 11   -   Accented Eighth Note Triplets with Bass Drum and Hi-Hat   45

Section 12   -   Drum Set Grooves   48

Section 13   -   Ride Cymbal Grooves and Four-Way Independence   52

Section 14   -   Hand Independence   56

Section 15   -   Bass Drum Independence   63

Section 16   -   Groove Independence   70

Section 17   -   Four-Way Independence   74

In Closing   78

BART ROBLEY's
SCHOOL OF
HARD ROCKS

The following is the key to reading the notation in this book.

Hi-Hat or Ride Cymbal   Snare Drum   Bass Drum   Hi-Hat Played with Left Foot

Learning music is like learning a new language. Not only do you need to learn how to speak the language, you need to learn how to read it as well. In music notation, counts are assigned to different notes, giving them each their own values. These notes are then put together to create rhythm.

This is much like the way letters are assigned different sounds and put together to form words. You must memorize these notes and their counts, or values, to know what sounds they make and the different ways they can be put together to form rhythms. If you can count it, you can play it!

Quarter Notes: 1   2   3   4   **Eighth Notes:** 1 & 2 & 3 & 4 &

Sixteenth Notes: 1 E & A 2 E & A 3 E & A 4 E & A

1 & A 2 & A 3 & A 4 & A 1 E & 2 E & 3 E & 4 E &

Eighth Note Triplets: 1 Trip Let 2 Trip Let 3 Trip Let 4 Trip Let

Introduction To Rhythm

Throughout this book, each numbered bar line is one exercise and should be repeated until you develop a groove. Practice to a click, starting out slow (between 70-80 B.P.M.), gradually pick-up the tempo as you develop a groove. This section is designed to teach the basics in reading rhythm by combining different quarter, eighth and sixteenth note combinations.

> The drive to create, perform and reproduce music is common to all mankind. A drive so basic that when a man cannot find an instrument to suit him, he creates his own.
>
> — Joseph Howard

29

30

31

32

33

34

35

SECTION TWO

Eighth Note Triplets

Now add eighth note triplets combined with different quarter, eighth and sixteenth note combinations.

Eighth Note Triplets

Eighth Note Triplets

Eighth Note Triplets

Eighth Note Triplets

Eighth Note Triplets

PHOTO: CALVIN LOWE

SECTION THREE

REBOUND STROKES

A double stroke roll is achieved when the drum stick rebounds off the drumhead, allowing it to only bounce two times. When learning how to do this, it is best to start by doubling eighth notes. Count the doubled eighth note as a sixteenth note. By the time you get to Exercise 12, you will have a controlled roll.

THE PREDOMINANT SOUND WE HEARD AS WE DEVELOPED IN THE WOMB WAS OUR MOTHERS' HEARTBEATS.... AS IT ANY WONDER THAT THE REPRODUCTION OF THESE PULSATIONS ALTERS OUR CONSCIOUSNESS AND HEIGHTENS OUR AWARENESS? OR REMINDS US WHAT WE ALREADY KNEWAND HAVE FORGOTTEN?

A. MANDALA

REBOUND STROKES

Rebound Sixteenth Notes

Once you have mastered doubling eighth notes, now try doubling sixteenth notes.

THE YAKUT SHAMAN PREFERS, FOR THE FRAME OF HIS DRUM, WOOD FROM A TREE THAT HAS BEEN STRUCK BY LIGHTNING.

~ ANDRE SCHAEFFNER ~

Rebound Sixteenth Notes

SECTION FIVE

WARM-UP EXERCISE

The following warm-up exercise combines sixteenth notes, 33 stroke rolls, 17 stroke rolls and 9 stroke rolls. This is a great exercise for warming up and getting ready to play.

The conquest of fear yields the courage of life. That is the cardinal initiation of every heroic adventure? Fearlessness and achievement.

— Joseph Campbell

Warm-up Exercise

SECTION SIX

Accented Sixteenth Notes

In this section, you will learn to play accents in a single measure of sixteenth notes. The accents will be displaced so that strong beats become weak and vice versa. This is called syncopation. When practicing these exercises, play the quarter notes on the Hi-Hat with your left foot. The quarter notes are the beat, the sixteenth notes are the division of time, and the accents are the syncopation.

"Drums are musical!
We knew that when we were little kids
playing on pots and pans."
Billy Ward
Inside Out - Exploring The
Mental Aspects of Drumming

Accented Sixteenth Notes

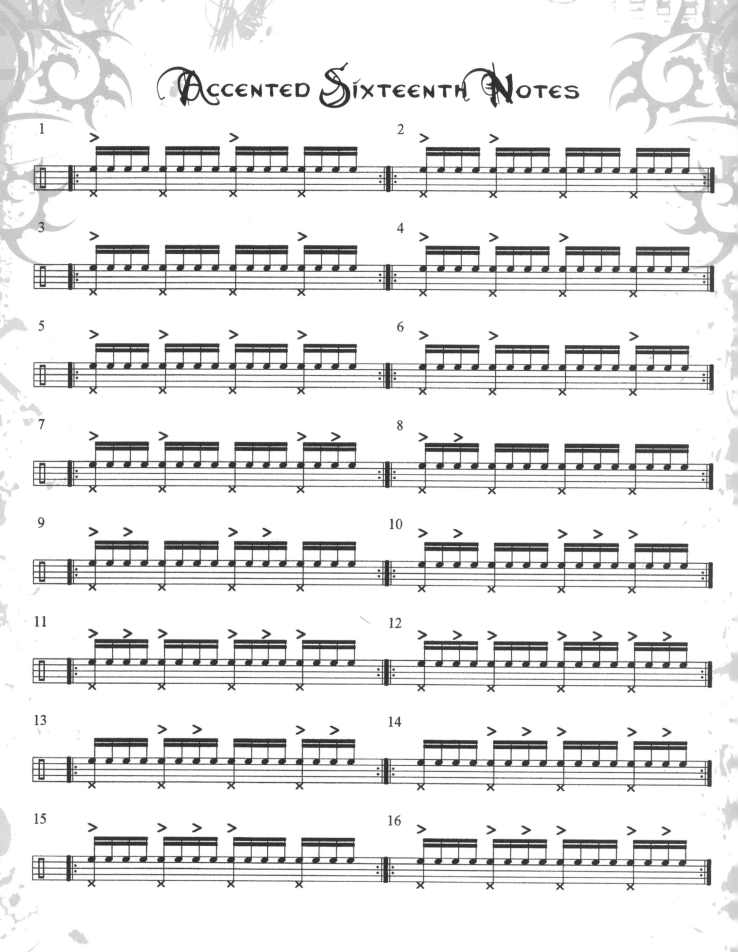

Accented Sixteenth Notes

17
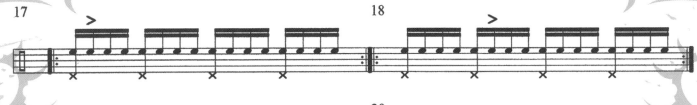

18

19
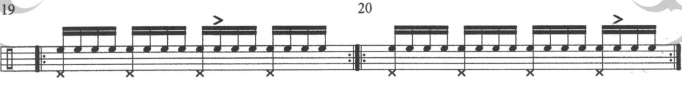

20

21
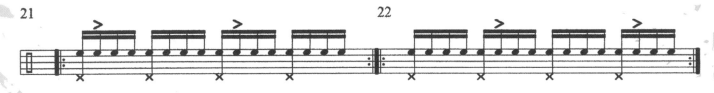

22

23

24

25
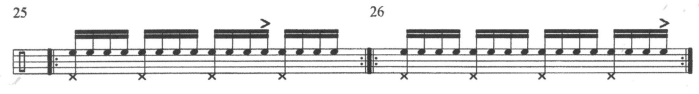

26

27
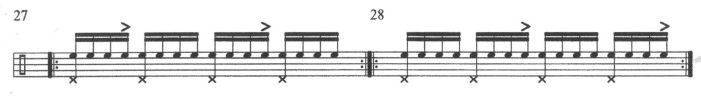

28

29
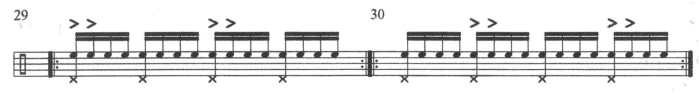

30

31
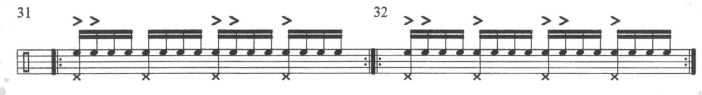

32

Accented Sixteenth Notes

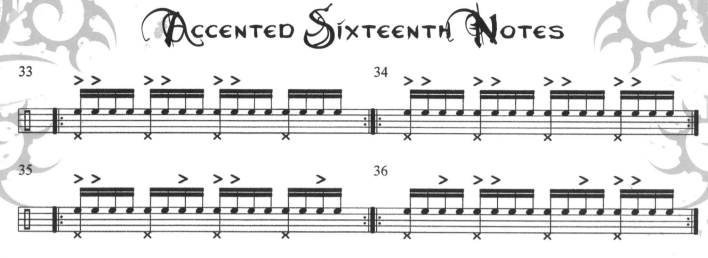

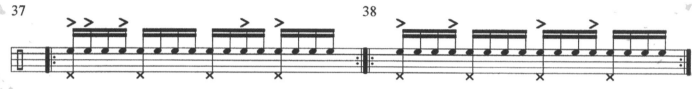

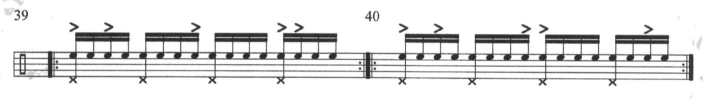

ACCENTED SIXTEENTH NOTES WITH BASS DRUM

Now that you have learned to put accents into a single bar of sixteenth notes, let's take it a step further. These exercises are the same as the previous section with two minor changes, the quarter note has been removed from the Hi-Hat and the Bass drum has been added to the accented notes.

"INSIDE OUR GUTS ARE WHEELS AND GEARS THAT COULD BE HELPING US WITH OUR TIMING— OR THEY CAN LIE DORMANT. I SAY GET OUT THE WD-40, GREASE'EM UP, AND TURN'EM LOOSE!"

— BILLY WARD —
*Inside Out - Exploring The
Mental Aspects of Drumming*

Accented Sixteenth Notes with Bass Drum

Accented Sixteenth Notes with Bass Drum

17

18

19

20

21

22

23

24

25

26

27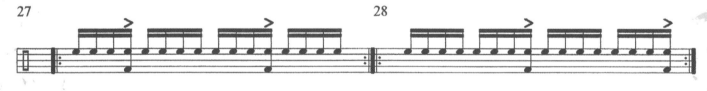

28

29

30

31

32

Accented Sixteenth Notes
with Bass Drum

Accented Sixteenth Notes with Hi-Hat and Bass Drum

Now that you have learned to put accents into a single bar of sixteenth notes, let's take it a step further. These exercises are the same as the previous section with two minor changes, the quarter note has been removed from the Hi-Hat and the Bass drum has been added to the accented notes.

A lot of drummers say they're self-taught. But we all learned from other drummers, whether we took lessons, went to concerts, or listened and played along with records. None of us is self-taught.

Gregg Bissonette
Modern Drummer Magazine
August 1998

Accented Sixteenth Notes with Hi-Hat and Bass Drum

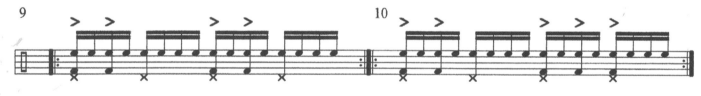

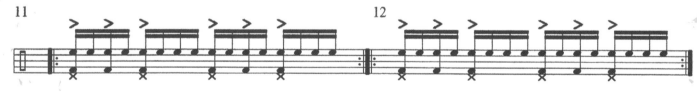

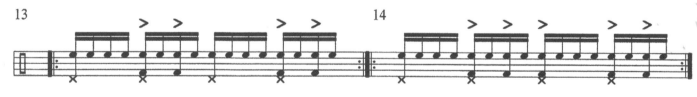

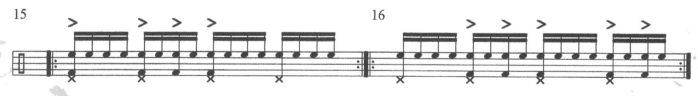

Accented Sixteenth Notes with Hi-Hat and Bass Drum

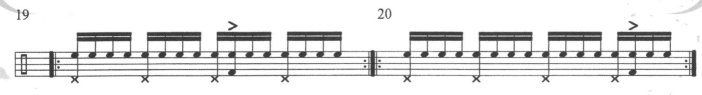

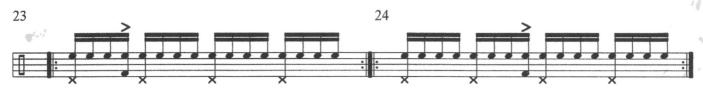

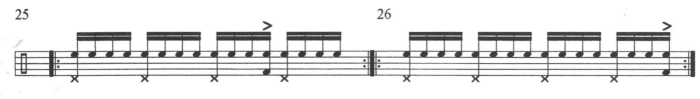

Accented Sixteenth Notes with Hi-Hat and Bass Drum

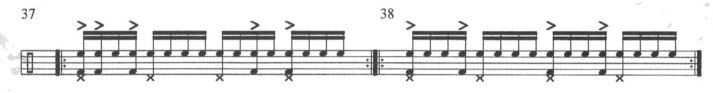

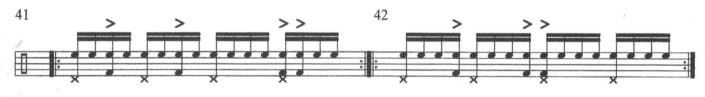

BART ROBLEY's

SCHOOL of HARD ROCKS

SECTION NINE

Accented Eighth Note Triplets

In this section you will learn to put accents into a single bar of eighth note triplets. As in the previous sections, play the quarter notes on the Hi-Hat with your left foot.

Every time you play the drums you should play like it's your last time.
~ Tommy Aldridge ~

Accented Eighth Note Triplets

Accented Eighth Note Triplets

BART ROBLEY's
SCHOOL OF
HARD ROCKS

SECTION TEN

Accented Eighth Note Triplets with Bass Drum

Now that you have learned to put accents into a single bar of eighth note triplets, take the same steps as you did in the sixteenth note sections. These exercises are the same as the previous section with two minor changes, the quarter note has been removed from the Hi-Hat and the Bass drum has been added to the accented notes.

Playing the drums is a great thing, after all, they are drums and you do get to hit them with sticks!

Bart Robley

Classic Drummer Magazine
July/August/September 2006

Bart Robley's

SCHOOL OF HARD ROCKS

Accented Eighth Note Triplets with Bass Drum

Accented Eighth Note Triplets with Bass Drum

Accented Eighth Note Triplets with Bass Drum and Hi-Hat

Let's take the final step. Now that you have added the Bass drum to the accented notes, add the quarter notes back to the Hi-Hat. Once you become comfortable and develop a groove, use your imagination and play the accented notes on the Tom Toms.

IF TEN VILLAGERS ARE BROUGHT TOGETHER TO WORK WITHOUT A MUSICIAN, NOTHING WILL BE ACCOMPLISHED. THE GROUP CHOOSES A MUSICIAN TO PLAY FOR THEM WHILE THEY WORK. THE PRODUCTIVITY OF THE GROUP DEPENDS ON THE MUSICIAN WHO ACCOMPANIES THEM. A SALARY INCREASE COULD NOT BE AS EFFECTIVE. WHIPPING WOULD ONLY PROVOKE REVOLT. A GOOD MUSICIAN BEHIND THE GROUP, WHO FOLLOWS THE RHYTHM OF EACH MEMBER, WILL HELP THEM ALL TO ACCELERATE. HIS PLAYING WILL MAKE THE WORK ENJOYABLE, OR AT LEAST LESS PAINFUL.

— YAYA DIALLO

BART ROBLEY's

SCHOOL OF HARD ROCKS

Accented Eighth Note Triplets with Bass Drum and Hi-Hat

Accented Eighth Note Triplets with Bass Drum and Hi-Hat

SECTION TWELVE

Drum Set Grooves

The following exercises are basic rock grooves which can be used in many playing situations. The top line represents the Hi-Hat, the second line the Snare drum, and the bottom line the Bass drum. Here you will learn to play with three-way coordination. When playing these grooves, picture your limbs working together. For instance, on count one where both the Hi-Hat and Bass drum are played simultaneously, your right hand and right foot should go up and down at the same time. The same rule applies to your hands. On counts two and four, where you play the Hi-Hat and Snare drum simultaneously, your hands should work together.

At the battle of Actium (31 B.C.) it is said that Queen Cleopatra used numerous sistra, played by women, to intimidate the enemy, giving rise to the appellation "Cleopatra's War Trumpet." It is difficult . . . to believe that the sound produced by a large body of women shaking such instruments could terrify a powerful foe.

— James Blades

BART ROBLEY's

SCHOOL OF HARD ROCKS

Drum Set Grooves

Drum Set Grooves

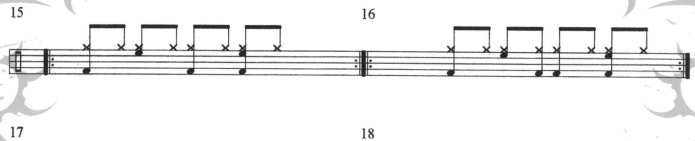

Drum Set Grooves

29

30

31

32

33

34

35
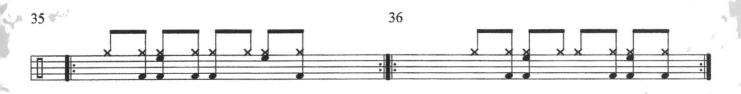

36

37

38

Ride Cymbal Grooves and Four-Way Independence

The following exercises are the same basic rock grooves discussed in the previous section. This time play the Ride cymbal instead of the Hi-Hat with your right hand, and add the quarter note to the Hi-Hat with your left foot. Once again, when playing these grooves, picture your limbs working together. Whenever two or more instruments are played simultaneously, those limbs should work together in an up and down motion.

These exercises should ultimately be mastered two ways, playing the Ride cymbal with the right hand and playing the quarter note with the left foot on the Hi-Hat. Then try playing the grooves holding the Hi-Hat closed with the ball of your left foot while tapping the heel of your left foot (think of it as standing on the tips of your toes). This will allow you to keep the Hi-Hat closed enabling you to play it with your right hand while continuing to keep the quarter note pulse with your left heel.

A good drummer listens
as much as he plays.
Indian Proverb

Ride Cymbal Grooves and Four-way Independence

Ride Cymbal Grooves and Four-way Independence

Ride Cymbal Grooves and Four-way Independence

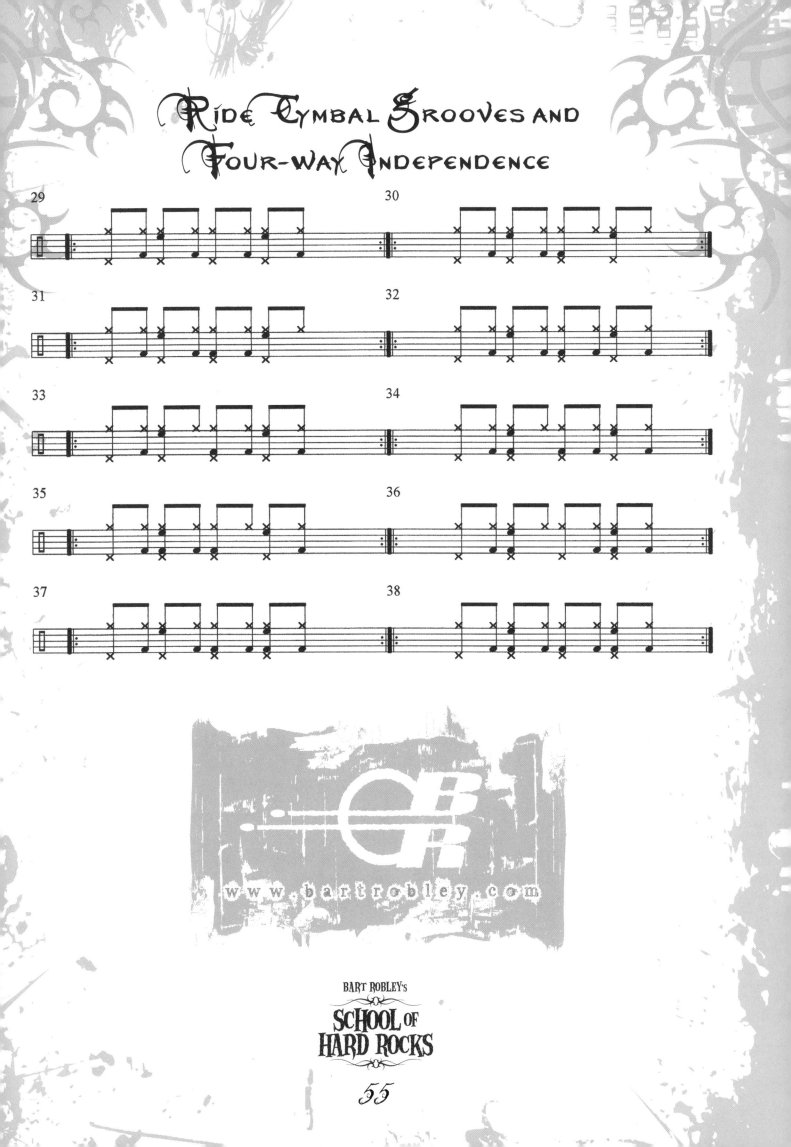

SECTION FOURTEEN

Hand Independence

Independence is achieved when you play two or more rhythms at the same time. In this section you will play the eighth notes with your right hand while playing the sixteenth notes with your left hand. The right hand can play the Hi-Hat or the Ride cymbal while your left hand plays the Snare drum. Once you become comfortable with these rhythms, use your imagination in moving your left hand around the Tom Toms.

A good groove releases adrenaline in your body. You feel uplifted, you feel centered, you feel calm, you feel powerful. You feel that energy. That's what good drumming is all about.
— Mickey Hart

Hand Independence

HAND INDEPENDENCE

81   82

83   84

85   86

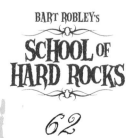

SECTION FIFTEEN

Bass Drum Independence

These are the same independence exercises as the previous section. However, you will use your right hand and right foot. Your right hand will play the Hi-Hat or Ride cymbal while your right foot plays the Bass drum.

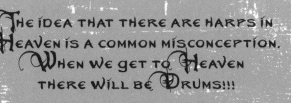

The idea that there are harps in Heaven is a common misconception. When we get to Heaven there will be Drums!!!
— Tony Vacca

Bass Drum Independence

Bass Drum Independence

BASS DRUM INDEPENDENCE

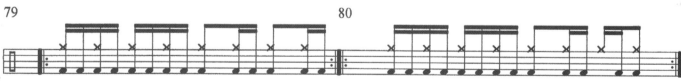

Bass Drum Independence

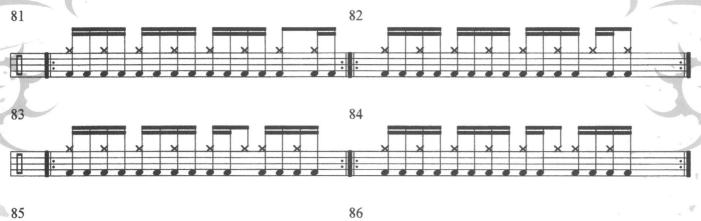

PHOTO: CYNDI MORRISON

SECTION SIXTEEN

Groove Independence

In this section you will take everything you have learned about independence between your hands and feet and combine them together into a groove. These rhythms can be challenging, so take your time, start slow, and repeat each measure until you develop a groove.

Rhythm is the soul of life.
The whole universe revolves in rhythm.
Every thing and every human action
revolves in rhythm.

— Baba Olatunji

BART ROBLEY's

SCHOOL OF HARD ROCKS

Groove Independence

1

2

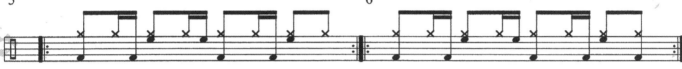

3

4

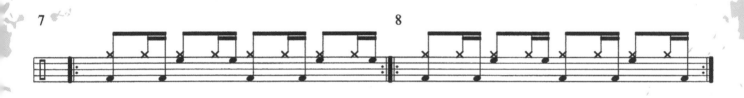

5

6

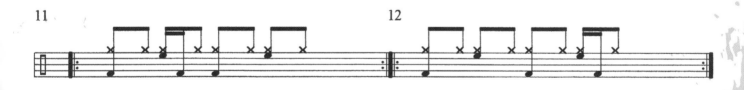

7

8

9

10

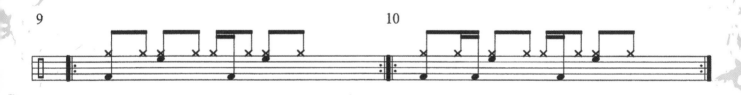

11

12

13

14

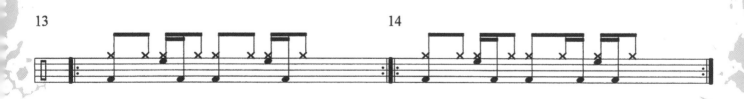

15

16

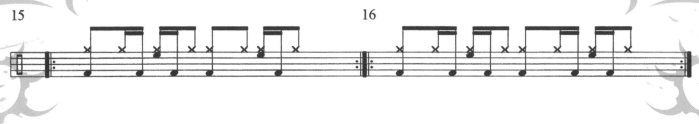

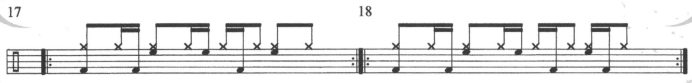

17

18

19

20

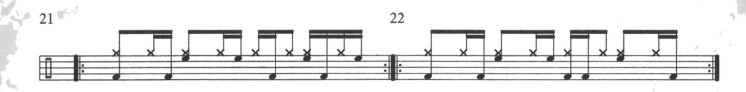

21

22

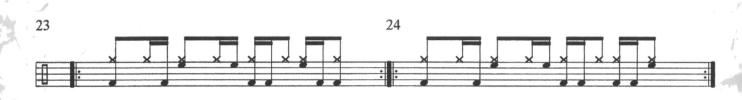

23

24

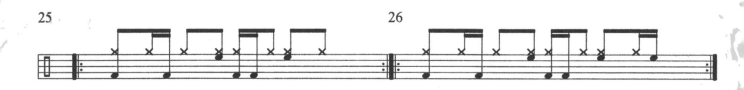

25

26

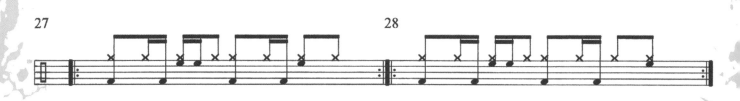

27

28

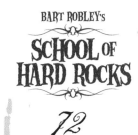

Groove Independence

29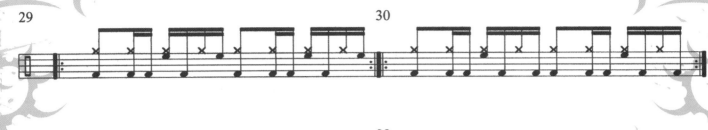

30

31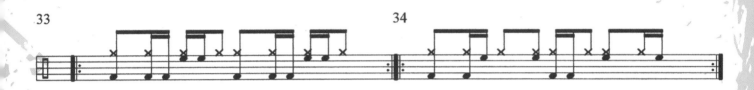

32

33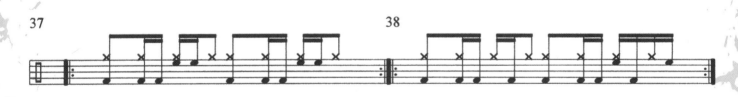

34

35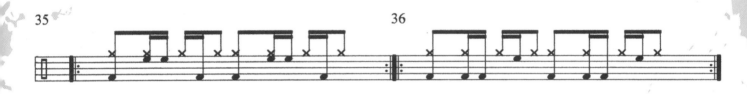

36

37

38

39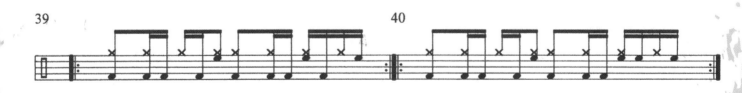

40

41

42

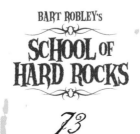

SECTION SEVENTEEN

Four-Way Independence

This section is the same as the previous section. However, this time you will add the quarter note in on the Hi-Hat. As in Section 13, each grove should be played two ways, the first way play the Ride cymbal with your right hand while playing the quarter note on the Hi-Hat. The second way is to hold the Hi-Hat closed with the ball of your left foot while tapping the quarter note with your left heel. This will enable you to play the Hi-Hat with your right hand, and continue to keep the quarter note pulse with your left heel.

It's been years and years and years i've been playing the drums, and they're still a challenge. I still enjoy using drumsticks and a snare drum.
— Charlie Watts

Four-Way Independence

1

2

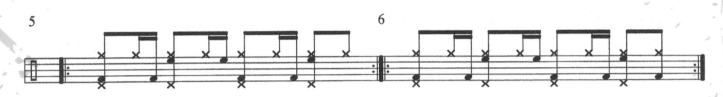

3

4

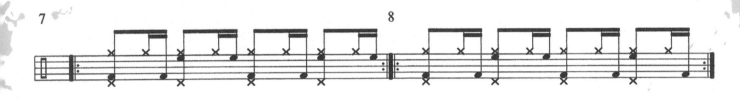

5

6

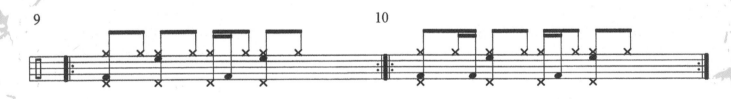

7

8

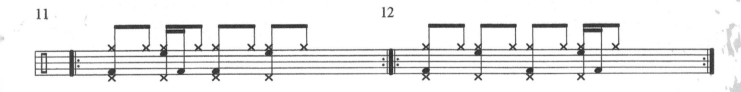

9

10

11

12

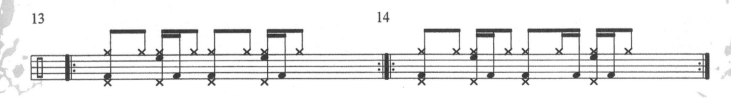

13

14

Four-Way Independence

15   16

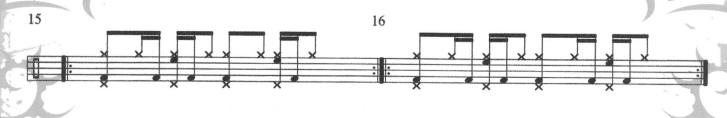

17   18

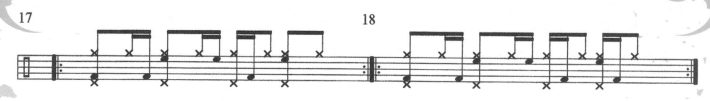

19   20

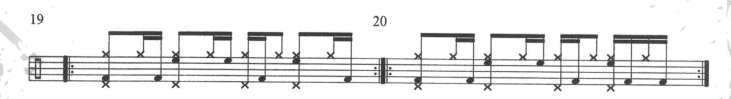

21   22

23   24

25   26

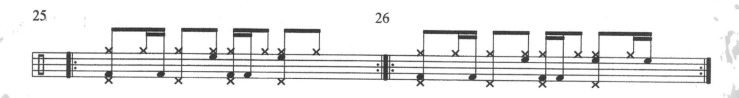

27   28

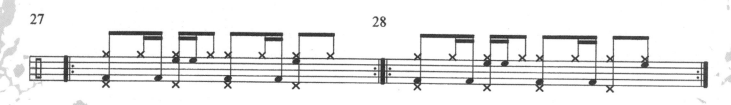

Four-way Independence

29 30
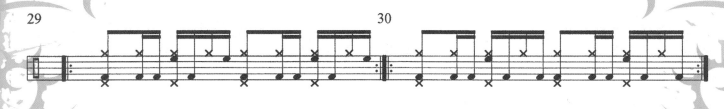

31 32
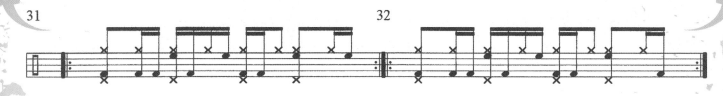

33 34
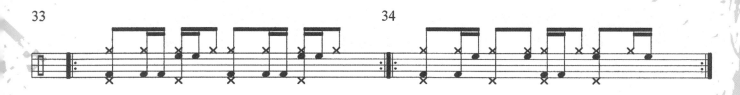

35 36
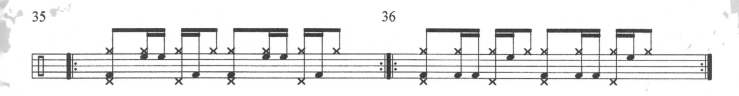

37 38
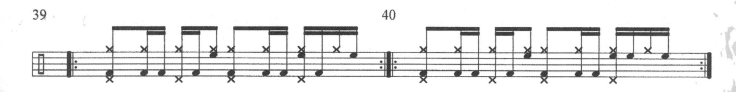

39 40
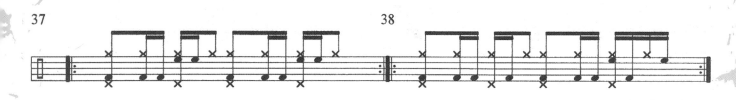

41 42
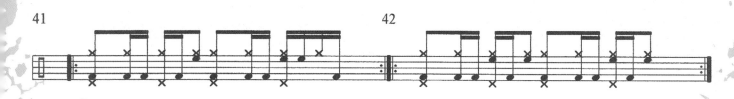

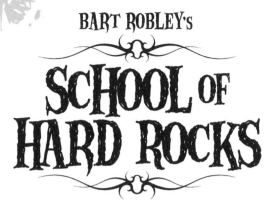

In Closing

I hope this book has been educational and helps your playing. I also hope it has been motivational and inspirational to everyone who plays through it. Writing this book has been something I have always wanted to do. It has been a great adventure and very educational as well.

I would like to thank the following people who have helped me in my drumming career and in the writing of this book: My wife Leah; Steve Cenker (E.T. #1); Sam Morrison; Greg Kasparian; Chris "The Doc" Daniels; Doreen Novotny; Mandy Burke; Cyndi Morrison; Dana Kasparian, Justin Novotny, Roy Dains; Allen Morgan; Roy Burns, Ron Marquez, Chris Brady, Gabe Diaz, Jamie Harris and everyone at Aquarian Drumheads; Billy Jeansonne and the entire staff at Classic Drummer Magazine; James Chudzinski of Symphonic Percussion; Mark Moralez of Kaman Percussion and Gretsch Drums; Michael Vail Blum of Titan Music, Inc.; Gregg Bissonette; Ralph Humphrey; Mo & Roger Palmateer and everyone at Mo's Fullerton Music... and to all of my students.

From the bottom of my heart, thank you!

Bart Robley

BART ENDORSES:

AQUARIAN DRUM HEADS

SYMPHONIC PERCUSSION
SOLID SHELL SNARE DRUMS

GLS MICS & CABLES

BART ALSO USES:

GRETSCH DRUMS

GIBRALTAR HARDWARE

ZILDJIAN CYMBALS

SPECIAL THANKS TO:
CLASSIC DRUMMER MAGAZINE
FOR THEIR UNDYING SUPPORT

Cover Design / Art Direction / Book Layout
Roy David Dains

 **London West**
ADVERTISING • DESIGN • ILLUSTRATION

www.londonwestadvertising.com

Great Percussion Books from Centerstream...